# *My*

# PTSD

# *Freedom Journal*

*My Journey In*

*Reclaiming Myself*

# Dedication

*My PTSD Journal Book is a result of my Bestest human friend in the whole wide universe told me from the core of their spirit. What I was hiding from and dealing with in denial. It was so taxing on our friendship, that they were making the decision of saying goodbye to our life long friendship. In that moment, it snapped me wide awake. Not from the threat of departure, but what they shared from the core of the spirit. What they experienced with their PSTD and how they were trying to overcome it. It was those deepen hidden experiences that I could relate to. And then going over my whole life experiences could relate to it 100+%. This is how this Journal and Book came into existence, because of their friendship love for me.*

*Truly Truly Truly Thank YOU!!!*

# Dedication

# Introduction

When I started to embark on my journey from PTSD, my best friend suggested to start a Journal and document my progress. So, at any time I can review my progress. I can see patterns.

Me loving to write and publish books, thought… BRILLANT! I can make *My PTSD Freedom Journal,* so that it encourages me while keeping myself accountable in this journey. Plus make it available, so others can do the same.

When I got done, I surprised my best with my first copy. And asked them to proof read it, while adding suggested content. *Their response was priceless 2.0.*

Here are some excerpts from that priceless conversation we had, that sparked embracing this journey…

12/02/25: *You are making up excuses. There's no point in talking about this because you are not going to actually see you are hindered and you don't have to live like this.*

*It's not mental dyslexia. You literally are putting up excuses. All these excuses and reasons, and none of it is accurate.*

12/03/25: *I don't care if you never wanna speak to me again after, but I'm concerned for you.*

…. (Then my "dyslexia" response).

*I care about you not that.*

That was the foundation for the format of this journal.

This is the foundation of My PTSD Freedom Journey:

**Before My Journey Begins:** Sets the tone and our mindset; of why we are journaling our way to being set free, from our PTSD.

**The Five Freedom Pillars:** Embracing the Five Characteristics of Unconditional Love for Myself. Throughout the five phases of my physical life. Being a child – faith and insight, an adult - perseverance, a friend - compassion, in a relationship – extrovert and as a parent – teaching others this cycle and being at peace with all the phases of my life. My book: *the Rosetta Stone of Unconditional Love* goes into greater details of the five characteristics of unconditional love; for ourselves and for others in our lives, with clarity.

**Daily Freedom Practice:** With the two previous mindset and foundations in place, we can now start journaling honestly about our experiences and reactions to them in two parts. Part One Morning/Day Journaling. And Part Two Night/Embracing and Letting go, before I go to Sleep Journaling.

**Weekly Review:** This is where I go back and review what I journaled this last week. My struggles, my patterns and my break throughs.

**Monthly Breakthrough:** This is where I go back and review over the last month my old wounds healing, my new strengths emerging and what I need to focus on next month.

and **My Freedom Letter:** Who I was, who I am now, who I refuse to be and who I choose to become… I am reclaiming what was always mine: my story, my voice, my peace and my future.

This journaling process allows me to be honest with myself. While being set free from all the repeated Past Traumas I experienced; that stole from me, who I really am and inspire to be.

**Ready? Here We Go…**

# Before My Journey Begins

**A note from my future self…**

*"I don't need to rush. Healing is not a race. Every breath I take is a step toward myself. I am reclaiming my life."*

(Write freely here)

______________________________________________

______________________________________________

______________________________________________

______________________________________________

______________________________________________

______________________________________________

______________________________________________

______________________________________________

______________________________________________

______________________________________________

______________________________________________

______________________________________________

## Why am I choosing Freedom

"Trauma tried to rewrite my story. I take the pen back and write my freedom."

## Who I'm Becoming

(Write freely here)

"I'm not defined by my past. I am who I choose to be now."

## What I Want My Life to Feel Like Again

(Write freely here)

“Peace isn’t the absent of memories – it is feeling safe within myself.”

# My Wounds I'm Ready to Acknowledge

(Write freely here)

"Acknowledging my pain is courage – it opens the doorway to my strength."

## My Hopes I'm Allowing Myself to Have

(Write freely here)

"Hopes do not deny reality. I declare that my reality still can change."

# The Five Freedom Pillars

*I breathe deeply. Each pillar is a place I can return to for support and growth.*

## 1. Safety – Returning to My Center

"Safety isn't a place. It's the permission I give myself to feel calm and secure."

(Suggestion. When writing our entries in our journals, try to write one liners. In this reflection prompt example, they would be like … 1. Away from crowds of people. 2. When connecting with nature and animals.

### Reflection Prompts:

***When do I feel*** the most safe?

________________________________________

________________________________________

________________________________________

________________________________________

***What situations make me feel unsafe,*** *and why?*

***What did safety feel like*** *in my childhood?*

***What does it feel*** *like now?*

***Where in my body do I feel*** *safety or tension?*

***What actions can I take daily to nurture** my sense of safety?*

## 2. Accountability Shame – Owning My Growth

"Growth begins when I release blame and step into awareness."

### Reflection Prompts:

***What patterns*** am I noticing in myself?

______________________________________________

______________________________________________

______________________________________________

______________________________________________

______________________________________________

______________________________________________

______________________________________________

______________________________________________

______________________________________________

______________________________________________

______________________________________________

______________________________________________

______________________________________________

______________________________________________

**When I react strongly,** what story am I telling myself?

***How can I support myself*** rather than judge myself?

***What small accomplishments*** can I celebrate today?

***What truth am I ready to face*** with gentleness?

## 3. Compassion for Self – Becoming My Own Friend.

"I speak to myself with kindness, as I would to a scared child."

### Reflection Prompts:

***What would I tell a friend*** in my situation?

**Where can I offer myself** compassion today?

***How have I minimized my pain,*** and why?

***What comforting words do I need to hear*** today?

***Where have I been too hard*** on myself?

## 4. Vulnerability in Safe Places – Opening the Door Slightly

"Vulnerability is my selective courage, not a weakness."

### Reflection Prompts:

***Who feels safe for me to share*** my truth with?

**Where can I allow myself to open up** a little more?

***What does healthy vulnerability look like*** for me?

***When did I last feel truly*** seen or heard?

***What small truth am I ready*** to express?

## 5. Legacy and Rebuilding – Who I Become From Here

"My future is mine to shape; I am not bound to my past."

**Reflection Prompts:**

***What life do I want to create from here?***

**What strengths has my trauma revealed?**

***What legacy do I want to have for myself?***

***Who is the version of me that no longer hides?***

***What does freedom feel like to me personally?***

# Daily Freedom Practice

"Healing happens in moments, one breath at a time."

**Day One: ___/___/______**

**MORNING JOURNALING:**

Today I felt trigger by:

______________________________________________

______________________________________________

______________________________________________

______________________________________________

______________________________________________

My body responded with:

______________________________________________

______________________________________________

______________________________________________

______________________________________________

______________________________________________

The root emotion I discovered was:

________________________________________

________________________________________

________________________________________

________________________________________

________________________________________

The truth behind that emotion is:

________________________________________

________________________________________

________________________________________

________________________________________

________________________________________

One thing I did today that showed strength was:

________________________________________

________________________________________

________________________________________

________________________________________

________________________________________

One small victory I'm celebrating is:

A message to my future self:

**EVENING CENTERING:**

"If all I did today was survive, I did enough"

Tonight my heart needs to hear:

One thing I can release before sleep is:

# Daily Freedom Practice

"Healing happens in moments, one breath at a time."

**Day Two: ___/___/______**

**MORNING JOURNALING:**

Today I felt trigger by:

My body responded with:

The root emotion I discovered was:

The truth behind that emotion is:

One thing I did today that showed strength was:

One small victory I'm celebrating is:

A message to my future self:

## EVENING CENTERING:

"If all I did today was survive, I did enough"

Tonight my heart needs to hear:

One thing I can release before sleep is:

# Daily Freedom Practice

"Healing happens in moments, one breath at a time."

**Day Three: ___/___/______**

**MORNING JOURNALING:**

Today I felt trigger by:

____________________________________________

____________________________________________

____________________________________________

____________________________________________

____________________________________________

My body responded with:

____________________________________________

____________________________________________

____________________________________________

____________________________________________

____________________________________________

The root emotion I discovered was:

The truth behind that emotion is:

One thing I did today that showed strength was:

One small victory I'm celebrating is:

________________________________________

________________________________________

________________________________________

________________________________________

________________________________________

A message to my future self:

________________________________________

________________________________________

________________________________________

________________________________________

________________________________________

**EVENING CENTERING:**

"If all I did today was survive, I did enough"

Tonight my heart needs to hear:

________________________________________

________________________________________

One thing I can release before sleep is:

# Daily Freedom Practice

"Healing happens in moments, one breath at a time."

**Day Four: ___/___/______**

**MORNING JOURNALING:**

Today I felt trigger by:

My body responded with:

The root emotion I discovered was:

The truth behind that emotion is:

One thing I did today that showed strength was:

One small victory I'm celebrating is:

A message to my future self:

## EVENING CENTERING:

"If all I did today was survive, I did enough"

Tonight my heart needs to hear:

One thing I can release before sleep is:

# Daily Freedom Practice

"Healing happens in moments, one breath at a time."

**Day Five: ___/___/______**

**MORNING JOURNALING:**

Today I felt trigger by:

_______________________________________________

_______________________________________________

_______________________________________________

_______________________________________________

_______________________________________________

My body responded with:

_______________________________________________

_______________________________________________

_______________________________________________

_______________________________________________

_______________________________________________

The root emotion I discovered was:

The truth behind that emotion is:

One thing I did today that showed strength was:

One small victory I'm celebrating is:

____________________________________________________________

A message to my future self:

**EVENING CENTERING:**

"If all I did today was survive, I did enough"

Tonight my heart needs to hear:

_______________________________________________

_______________________________________________

_______________________________________________

_______________________________________________

_______________________________________________

One thing I can release before sleep is:

_______________________________________________

_______________________________________________

_______________________________________________

_______________________________________________

_______________________________________________

# Daily Freedom Practice

"Healing happens in moments, one breath at a time."

**Day Six: ___/___/______**

**MORNING JOURNALING:**

Today I felt trigger by:

My body responded with:

The root emotion I discovered was:

The truth behind that emotion is:

________________________________________

________________________________________

________________________________________

________________________________________

________________________________________

One thing I did today that showed strength was:

________________________________________

________________________________________

________________________________________

________________________________________

________________________________________

One small victory I’m celebrating is:

________________________________________

________________________________________

________________________________________

________________________________________

________________________________________

A message to my future self:

**EVENING CENTERING:**

"If all I did today was survive, I did enough"

Tonight my heart needs to hear:

One thing I can release before sleep is:

______________________________________________

______________________________________________

______________________________________________

# Daily Freedom Practice

"Healing happens in moments, one breath at a time."

**Day Seven: ___/___/______**

**MORNING JOURNALING:**

Today I felt trigger by:

______________________________________________

______________________________________________

______________________________________________

______________________________________________

______________________________________________

My body responded with:

______________________________________________

______________________________________________

The root emotion I discovered was:

The truth behind that emotion is:

One thing I did today that showed strength was:

One small victory I'm celebrating is:

A message to my future self:

**EVENING CENTERING:**

"If all I did today was survive, I did enough"

Tonight my heart needs to hear:

______________________________________________

______________________________________________

______________________________________________

______________________________________________

______________________________________________

One thing I can release before sleep is:

______________________________________________

______________________________________________

______________________________________________

______________________________________________

______________________________________________

# Weekly Review

"Healing becomes visible when I reflect on my journey."

What did I handle better than last week?

What pattern am I starting to understand?

What part of myself came back online this week?

One old wound that softened this week:

One new strength that appeared:

One thing I'm grateful I didn't give up on:

# Daily Freedom Practice

"Healing happens in moments, one breath at a time."

**Day Eight: ___/___/_____**

**MORNING JOURNALING:**

Today I felt trigger by:

_______________________________________________

_______________________________________________

_______________________________________________

_______________________________________________

_______________________________________________

My body responded with:

_______________________________________________

_______________________________________________

_______________________________________________

The root emotion I discovered was:

The truth behind that emotion is:

One thing I did today that showed strength was:

One small victory I'm celebrating is:

A message to my future self:

**EVENING CENTERING:**

"If all I did today was survive, I did enough"

Tonight my heart needs to hear:

____________________________________________

____________________________________________

____________________________________________

____________________________________________

____________________________________________

One thing I can release before sleep is:

____________________________________________

____________________________________________

____________________________________________

____________________________________________

____________________________________________

# Daily Freedom Practice

"Healing happens in moments, one breath at a time."

**Day Nine: ___/___/______**

**MORNING JOURNALING:**

Today I felt trigger by:

My body responded with:

The root emotion I discovered was:

The truth behind that emotion is:

One thing I did today that showed strength was:

One small victory I'm celebrating is:

A message to my future self:

## EVENING CENTERING:

"If all I did today was survive, I did enough"

Tonight my heart needs to hear:

One thing I can release before sleep is:

______________________________________________

______________________________________________

# Daily Freedom Practice

"Healing happens in moments, one breath at a time."

**Day Ten: ___/___/______**

**MORNING JOURNALING:**

Today I felt trigger by:

______________________________________________

______________________________________________

______________________________________________

______________________________________________

______________________________________________

My body responded with:

______________________________________________

______________________________________________

______________________________________________

The root emotion I discovered was:

The truth behind that emotion is:

One thing I did today that showed strength was:

One small victory I'm celebrating is:

A message to my future self:

**EVENING CENTERING:**

"If all I did today was survive, I did enough"

Tonight my heart needs to hear:

One thing I can release before sleep is:

# Daily Freedom Practice

"Healing happens in moments, one breath at a time."

**Day Eleven: ___/___/______**

**MORNING JOURNALING:**

Today I felt trigger by:

My body responded with:

The root emotion I discovered was:

The truth behind that emotion is:

One thing I did today that showed strength was:

One small victory I'm celebrating is:

A message to my future self:

## EVENING CENTERING:

"If all I did today was survive, I did enough"

Tonight my heart needs to hear:

One thing I can release before sleep is:

______________________________________________

______________________________________________

# Daily Freedom Practice

"Healing happens in moments, one breath at a time."

**Day Twelve: ___/___/_____**

**MORNING JOURNALING:**

Today I felt trigger by:

______________________________________________

______________________________________________

______________________________________________

______________________________________________

______________________________________________

My body responded with:

______________________________________________

______________________________________________

______________________________________________

The root emotion I discovered was:

The truth behind that emotion is:

One thing I did today that showed strength was:

One small victory I'm celebrating is:

A message to my future self:

**EVENING CENTERING:**

"If all I did today was survive, I did enough"

Tonight my heart needs to hear:

_______________________________________________

_______________________________________________

_______________________________________________

_______________________________________________

_______________________________________________

One thing I can release before sleep is:

_______________________________________________

_______________________________________________

_______________________________________________

_______________________________________________

_______________________________________________

# Daily Freedom Practice

"Healing happens in moments, one breath at a time."

**Day Thirteen: ___/___/______**

# MORNING JOURNALING:

Today I felt trigger by:

My body responded with:

The root emotion I discovered was:

The truth behind that emotion is:

One thing I did today that showed strength was:

One small victory I'm celebrating is:

A message to my future self:

**EVENING CENTERING:**

"If all I did today was survive, I did enough"

Tonight my heart needs to hear:

One thing I can release before sleep is:

_______________________________________________

_______________________________________________

_______________________________________________

_______________________________________________

_______________________________________________

# Daily Freedom Practice:

## Day Fourteen: ___/___/______

### MORNING JOURNALING:

Today I felt trigger by:

_______________________________________________

_______________________________________________

_______________________________________________

_______________________________________________

_______________________________________________

My body responded with:

The root emotion I discovered was:

The truth behind that emotion is:

One thing I did today that showed strength was:

_______________________________________________

_______________________________________________

_______________________________________________

_______________________________________________

_______________________________________________

One small victory I'm celebrating is:

_______________________________________________

_______________________________________________

_______________________________________________

_______________________________________________

_______________________________________________

A message to my future self:

_______________________________________________

_______________________________________________

_______________________________________________

_______________________________________________

_______________________________________________

**EVENING CENTERING:**

"If all I did today was survive, I did enough"

Tonight my heart needs to hear:

________________________________________

________________________________________

________________________________________

________________________________________

________________________________________

One thing I can release before sleep is:

________________________________________

________________________________________

________________________________________

________________________________________

________________________________________

# Weekly Review

"Healing becomes visible when I reflect on my journey."

What did I handle better than last week?

_______________________________________________

_______________________________________________

_______________________________________________

_______________________________________________

_______________________________________________

What pattern am I starting to understand?

_______________________________________________

_______________________________________________

_______________________________________________

_______________________________________________

_______________________________________________

What part of myself came back online this week?

_______________________________________________

_______________________________________________

One old wound that softened this week:

One new strength that appeared:

One thing I'm grateful I didn't give up on:

______________________________________________

______________________________________________

______________________________________________

# Daily Freedom Practice

"Healing happens in moments, one breath at a time."

**Day Fifteen: ___/___/______**

**MORNING JOURNALING:**

Today I felt trigger by:

______________________________________________

______________________________________________

______________________________________________

______________________________________________

______________________________________________

My body responded with:

The root emotion I discovered was:

The truth behind that emotion is:

One thing I did today that showed strength was:

One small victory I'm celebrating is:

A message to my future self:

**EVENING CENTERING:**

"If all I did today was survive, I did enough"

Tonight my heart needs to hear:

______________________________________________

______________________________________________

______________________________________________

______________________________________________

______________________________________________

One thing I can release before sleep is:

______________________________________________

______________________________________________

______________________________________________

______________________________________________

______________________________________________

# Daily Freedom Practice

"Healing happens in moments, one breath at a time."

**Day Sixteen: ___/___/_____**

**MORNING JOURNALING:**

Today I felt trigger by:

________________________________________________

________________________________________________

________________________________________________

________________________________________________

________________________________________________

My body responded with:

________________________________________________

________________________________________________

________________________________________________

________________________________________________

________________________________________________

The root emotion I discovered was:

________________________________________________

________________________________________________

The truth behind that emotion is:

One thing I did today that showed strength was:

One small victory I'm celebrating is:

A message to my future self:

**EVENING CENTERING:**

“If all I did today was survive, I did enough”

Tonight my heart needs to hear:

One thing I can release before sleep is:

______________________________________________

______________________________________________

______________________________________________

______________________________________________

______________________________________________

# Daily Freedom Practice

"Healing happens in moments, one breath at a time."

**Day Seventeen: ___/___/______**

**MORNING JOURNALING:**

Today I felt trigger by:

______________________________________________

______________________________________________

______________________________________________

______________________________________________

______________________________________________

My body responded with:

________________________________________________

The root emotion I discovered was:

The truth behind that emotion is:

One thing I did today that showed strength was:

One small victory I'm celebrating is:

A message to my future self:

## EVENING CENTERING:

"If all I did today was survive, I did enough"

Tonight my heart needs to hear:

________________________________________________

________________________________________________

________________________________________________

________________________________________________

________________________________________________

One thing I can release before sleep is:

________________________________________________

________________________________________________

________________________________________________

________________________________________________

________________________________________________

# Daily Freedom Practice

"Healing happens in moments, one breath at a time."

## Day Eighteen: ___/___/______

## MORNING JOURNALING:

Today I felt trigger by:

______________________________________________

______________________________________________

______________________________________________

______________________________________________

______________________________________________

My body responded with:

______________________________________________

______________________________________________

______________________________________________

______________________________________________

______________________________________________

The root emotion I discovered was:

______________________________________________

______________________________________________

The truth behind that emotion is:

One thing I did today that showed strength was:

One small victory I'm celebrating is:

A message to my future self:

**EVENING CENTERING:**

"If all I did today was survive, I did enough"

Tonight my heart needs to hear:

One thing I can release before sleep is:

___

___

___

___

___

# Daily Freedom Practice

"Healing happens in moments, one breath at a time."

**Day Nineteen: ___/___/______**

**MORNING JOURNALING:**

Today I felt trigger by:

___

___

___

___

___

My body responded with:

________________________________________

________________________________________

________________________________________

________________________________________

________________________________________

The root emotion I discovered was:

________________________________________

________________________________________

________________________________________

________________________________________

________________________________________

The truth behind that emotion is:

________________________________________

________________________________________

________________________________________

________________________________________

________________________________________

One thing I did today that showed strength was:

________________________________________

One small victory I'm celebrating is:

A message to my future self:

## EVENING CENTERING:

"If all I did today was survive, I did enough"

Tonight my heart needs to hear:

______________________________________________

______________________________________________

______________________________________________

______________________________________________

______________________________________________

One thing I can release before sleep is:

______________________________________________

______________________________________________

______________________________________________

______________________________________________

______________________________________________

# Daily Freedom Practice

"Healing happens in moments, one breath at a time."

**Day Twenty: ___/___/______**

**MORNING JOURNALING:**

Today I felt trigger by:

______________________________________________________________

______________________________________________________________

______________________________________________________________

______________________________________________________________

______________________________________________________________

My body responded with:

______________________________________________________________

______________________________________________________________

______________________________________________________________

______________________________________________________________

______________________________________________________________

The root emotion I discovered was:

______________________________________

______________________________________

______________________________________

______________________________________

______________________________________

The truth behind that emotion is:

______________________________________

______________________________________

______________________________________

______________________________________

______________________________________

One thing I did today that showed strength was:

______________________________________

______________________________________

______________________________________

______________________________________

______________________________________

One small victory I'm celebrating is:

_______________________________________________

_______________________________________________

_______________________________________________

_______________________________________________

_______________________________________________

A message to my future self:

_______________________________________________

_______________________________________________

_______________________________________________

_______________________________________________

_______________________________________________

**EVENING CENTERING:**

"If all I did today was survive, I did enough"

Tonight my heart needs to hear:

_______________________________________________

_______________________________________________

One thing I can release before sleep is:

# Daily Freedom Practice

"Healing happens in moments, one breath at a time."

**Day Twenty-One: ___/___/______**

## MORNING JOURNALING:

Today I felt trigger by:

My body responded with:

The root emotion I discovered was:

The truth behind that emotion is:

One thing I did today that showed strength was:

One small victory I'm celebrating is:

A message to my future self:

## EVENING CENTERING:

"If all I did today was survive, I did enough"

Tonight my heart needs to hear:

One thing I can release before sleep is:

# Weekly Review

"Healing becomes visible when I reflect on my journey."

What did I handle better than last week?

What pattern am I starting to understand?

What part of myself came back online this week?

________________________________________

________________________________________

________________________________________

________________________________________

________________________________________

One old wound that softened this week:

________________________________________

________________________________________

________________________________________

________________________________________

________________________________________

One new strength that appeared:

________________________________________

________________________________________

________________________________________

________________________________________

________________________________________

One thing I'm grateful I didn't give up on:

___

___

___

___

___

# Daily Freedom Practice

"Healing happens in moments, one breath at a time."

**Day Twenty-Two: ___/___/______**

**MORNING JOURNALING:**

Today I felt trigger by:

___

___

___

My body responded with:

The root emotion I discovered was:

The truth behind that emotion is:

One thing I did today that showed strength was:

One small victory I'm celebrating is:

A message to my future self:

**EVENING CENTERING:**

"If all I did today was survive, I did enough"

Tonight my heart needs to hear:

One thing I can release before sleep is:

# Daily Freedom Practice

"Healing happens in moments, one breath at a time."

**Day Twenty-Three: ___/___/______**

**MORNING JOURNALING:**

Today I felt trigger by:

______________________________________________

______________________________________________

______________________________________________

______________________________________________

______________________________________________

My body responded with:

______________________________________________

______________________________________________

______________________________________________

______________________________________________

______________________________________________

The root emotion I discovered was:

The truth behind that emotion is:

One thing I did today that showed strength was:

One small victory I'm celebrating is:

A message to my future self:

**EVENING CENTERING:**

"If all I did today was survive, I did enough"

Tonight my heart needs to hear:

One thing I can release before sleep is:

# Daily Freedom Practice

"Healing happens in moments, one breath at a time."

**Day Twenty-Four: ___/___/______**

**MORNING JOURNALING:**

Today I felt trigger by:

My body responded with:

The root emotion I discovered was:

The truth behind that emotion is:

One thing I did today that showed strength was:

One small victory I'm celebrating is:

A message to my future self:

## EVENING CENTERING:

"If all I did today was survive, I did enough"

Tonight my heart needs to hear:

One thing I can release before sleep is:

# Daily Freedom Practice

"Healing happens in moments, one breath at a time."

**Day Twenty-Five: ___/___/______**

**MORNING JOURNALING:**

Today I felt trigger by:

________________________________________________

________________________________________________

________________________________________________

________________________________________________

________________________________________________

My body responded with:

________________________________________________

________________________________________________

________________________________________________

________________________________________________

________________________________________________

The root emotion I discovered was:

The truth behind that emotion is:

One thing I did today that showed strength was:

One small victory I'm celebrating is:

_______________________________________________

_______________________________________________

_______________________________________________

_______________________________________________

_______________________________________________

A message to my future self:

_______________________________________________

_______________________________________________

_______________________________________________

_______________________________________________

_______________________________________________

**EVENING CENTERING:**

"If all I did today was survive, I did enough"

Tonight my heart needs to hear:

One thing I can release before sleep is:

# Daily Freedom Practice

"Healing happens in moments, one breath at a time."

**Day Twenty-Six: ___/___/______**

**MORNING JOURNALING:**

Today I felt trigger by:

My body responded with:

The root emotion I discovered was:

The truth behind that emotion is:

One thing I did today that showed strength was:

One small victory I'm celebrating is:

A message to my future self:

## EVENING CENTERING:

"If all I did today was survive, I did enough"

Tonight my heart needs to hear:

One thing I can release before sleep is:

_______________________________________________

_______________________________________________

# Daily Freedom Practice

"Healing happens in moments, one breath at a time."

**Day Twenty-Seven: ___/___/______**

**MORNING JOURNALING:**

Today I felt trigger by:

_______________________________________________

_______________________________________________

_______________________________________________

_______________________________________________

_______________________________________________

My body responded with:

The root emotion I discovered was:

The truth behind that emotion is:

One thing I did today that showed strength was:

One small victory I'm celebrating is:

A message to my future self:

**EVENING CENTERING:**

"If all I did today was survive, I did enough"

Tonight my heart needs to hear:

_______________________________________________

_______________________________________________

_______________________________________________

_______________________________________________

_______________________________________________

One thing I can release before sleep is:

_______________________________________________

_______________________________________________

_______________________________________________

_______________________________________________

_______________________________________________

# Daily Freedom Practice

"Healing happens in moments, one breath at a time."

## Day Twenty-Eight: ___/___/______

### MORNING JOURNALING:

Today I felt trigger by:

______________________________________________

______________________________________________

______________________________________________

______________________________________________

______________________________________________

My body responded with:

______________________________________________

______________________________________________

______________________________________________

______________________________________________

______________________________________________

The root emotion I discovered was:

______________________________________________

______________________________________________

The truth behind that emotion is:

One thing I did today that showed strength was:

One small victory I'm celebrating is:

A message to my future self:

**EVENING CENTERING:**

"If all I did today was survive, I did enough"

Tonight my heart needs to hear:

One thing I can release before sleep is:

____________________________________________

____________________________________________

____________________________________________

____________________________________________

____________________________________________

# Weekly Review

“Healing becomes visible when I reflect on my journey.”

What did I handle better than last week?

____________________________________________

____________________________________________

____________________________________________

____________________________________________

____________________________________________

What pattern am I starting to understand?

________________________________________

What part of myself came back online this week?

One old wound that softened this week:

One new strength that appeared:

____________________________________________

____________________________________________

____________________________________________

____________________________________________

____________________________________________

One thing I'm grateful I didn't give up on:

____________________________________________

____________________________________________

____________________________________________

____________________________________________

____________________________________________

# 1st Monthly Breakthrough Page

"Breakthroughs are quiet moments of clarity. Not explosions."

What I see changing in me:

Old wounds that shifted:

New strengths I'm noticing:

People who feel safe for me now:

People I am learning to distance from:

My biggest win this month:

________________________________________

________________________________________

What I want to focus on next month:

________________________________________

________________________________________

________________________________________

________________________________________

________________________________________

# Daily Freedom Practice

"Healing happens in moments, one breath at a time."

**Day One: ___/___/______**

**MORNING JOURNALING:**

Today I felt trigger by:

My body responded with:

The root emotion I discovered was:

The truth behind that emotion is:

One thing I did today that showed strength was:

One small victory I'm celebrating is:

A message to my future self:

**EVENING CENTERING:**

"If all I did today was survive, I did enough"

Tonight my heart needs to hear:

One thing I can release before sleep is:

# Daily Freedom Practice

"Healing happens in moments, one breath at a time."

**Day Two: ___/___/______**

**MORNING JOURNALING:**

Today I felt trigger by:

My body responded with:

The root emotion I discovered was:

The truth behind that emotion is:

One thing I did today that showed strength was:

One small victory I'm celebrating is:

A message to my future self:

**EVENING CENTERING:**

"If all I did today was survive, I did enough"

Tonight my heart needs to hear:

One thing I can release before sleep is:

# Daily Freedom Practice

"Healing happens in moments, one breath at a time."

**Day Three: ___/___/______**

**MORNING JOURNALING:**

Today I felt trigger by:

My body responded with:

The root emotion I discovered was:

The truth behind that emotion is:

One thing I did today that showed strength was:

One small victory I'm celebrating is:

A message to my future self:

## EVENING CENTERING:

"If all I did today was survive, I did enough"

Tonight my heart needs to hear:

One thing I can release before sleep is:

______________________________________________

______________________________________________

# Daily Freedom Practice

"Healing happens in moments, one breath at a time."

**Day Four: ___/___/______**

**MORNING JOURNALING:**

Today I felt trigger by:

______________________________________________

______________________________________________

______________________________________________

______________________________________________

______________________________________________

My body responded with:

______________________________________________

______________________________________________

______________________________________________

The root emotion I discovered was:

The truth behind that emotion is:

One thing I did today that showed strength was:

One small victory I'm celebrating is:

A message to my future self:

**EVENING CENTERING:**

"If all I did today was survive, I did enough"

Tonight my heart needs to hear:

_______________________________________________

_______________________________________________

_______________________________________________

_______________________________________________

_______________________________________________

One thing I can release before sleep is:

_______________________________________________

_______________________________________________

_______________________________________________

_______________________________________________

_______________________________________________

# Daily Freedom Practice

"Healing happens in moments, one breath at a time."

**Day Five: ___/___/______**

**MORNING JOURNALING:**

Today I felt trigger by:

____________________________________________________________

My body responded with:

The root emotion I discovered was:

The truth behind that emotion is:

________________________________________

________________________________________

________________________________________

________________________________________

________________________________________

One thing I did today that showed strength was:

________________________________________

________________________________________

________________________________________

________________________________________

________________________________________

One small victory I’m celebrating is:

________________________________________

________________________________________

________________________________________

________________________________________

________________________________________

A message to my future self:

______________________________________________

______________________________________________

______________________________________________

______________________________________________

______________________________________________

## EVENING CENTERING:

"If all I did today was survive, I did enough"

Tonight my heart needs to hear:

______________________________________________

______________________________________________

______________________________________________

______________________________________________

______________________________________________

One thing I can release before sleep is:

______________________________________________

______________________________________________

___________________________________________

___________________________________________

___________________________________________

# Daily Freedom Practice

"Healing happens in moments, one breath at a time."

**Day Six: ___/___/_____**

**MORNING JOURNALING:**

Today I felt trigger by:

___________________________________________

___________________________________________

___________________________________________

___________________________________________

___________________________________________

My body responded with:

The root emotion I discovered was:

The truth behind that emotion is:

One thing I did today that showed strength was:

______________________________________________________________________________________________________________________________

One small victory I'm celebrating is:

A message to my future self:

**EVENING CENTERING:**

"If all I did today was survive, I did enough"

Tonight my heart needs to hear:

________________________________________

________________________________________

________________________________________

________________________________________

________________________________________

One thing I can release before sleep is:

________________________________________

________________________________________

________________________________________

________________________________________

________________________________________

# Daily Freedom Practice

"Healing happens in moments, one breath at a time."

**Day Seven: ___/___/_____**

**MORNING JOURNALING:**

Today I felt trigger by:

________________________________________________

________________________________________________

________________________________________________

________________________________________________

________________________________________________

My body responded with:

________________________________________________

________________________________________________

________________________________________________

________________________________________________

________________________________________________

The root emotion I discovered was:

________________________________________________

________________________________________________

The truth behind that emotion is:

One thing I did today that showed strength was:

One small victory I'm celebrating is:

A message to my future self:

**EVENING CENTERING:**

"If all I did today was survive, I did enough"

Tonight my heart needs to hear:

One thing I can release before sleep is:

______________________________________________

______________________________________________

______________________________________________

______________________________________________

______________________________________________

# Weekly Review

“Healing becomes visible when I reflect on my journey.”

What did I handle better than last week?

______________________________________________

______________________________________________

______________________________________________

______________________________________________

______________________________________________

What pattern am I starting to understand?

______________________________________________

______________________________________________

______________________________________________

______________________________________________

______________________________________________

What part of myself came back online this week?

______________________________________________

______________________________________________

______________________________________________

______________________________________________

______________________________________________

One old wound that softened this week:

______________________________________________

______________________________________________

______________________________________________

______________________________________________

______________________________________________

One new strength that appeared:

________________________________________

________________________________________

________________________________________

________________________________________

________________________________________

One thing I'm grateful I didn't give up on:

________________________________________

________________________________________

________________________________________

________________________________________

________________________________________

# Daily Freedom Practice

"Healing happens in moments, one breath at a time."

**Day Eight: ___/___/______**

## MORNING JOURNALING:

Today I felt trigger by:

My body responded with:

The root emotion I discovered was:

The truth behind that emotion is:

One thing I did today that showed strength was:

One small victory I'm celebrating is:

A message to my future self:

**EVENING CENTERING:**

"If all I did today was survive, I did enough"

Tonight my heart needs to hear:

One thing I can release before sleep is:

_______________________________________________

_______________________________________________

_______________________________________________

_______________________________________________

_______________________________________________

# Daily Freedom Practice

"Healing happens in moments, one breath at a time."

**Day Nine: ___/___/______**

**MORNING JOURNALING:**

Today I felt trigger by:

_______________________________________________

_______________________________________________

_______________________________________________

_______________________________________________

_______________________________________________

My body responded with:

The root emotion I discovered was:

The truth behind that emotion is:

One thing I did today that showed strength was:

________________________________________

________________________________________

________________________________________

________________________________________

________________________________________

One small victory I’m celebrating is:

________________________________________

________________________________________

________________________________________

________________________________________

________________________________________

A message to my future self:

________________________________________

________________________________________

________________________________________

________________________________________

________________________________________

## EVENING CENTERING:

"If all I did today was survive, I did enough"

Tonight my heart needs to hear:

________________________________________

________________________________________

________________________________________

________________________________________

________________________________________

One thing I can release before sleep is:

________________________________________

________________________________________

________________________________________

________________________________________

________________________________________

# Daily Freedom Practice

"Healing happens in moments, one breath at a time."

**Day Ten: ___/___/______**

**MORNING JOURNALING:**

Today I felt trigger by:

______________________________________________

______________________________________________

______________________________________________

______________________________________________

______________________________________________

My body responded with:

______________________________________________

______________________________________________

______________________________________________

______________________________________________

______________________________________________

The root emotion I discovered was:

______________________________________________

______________________________________________

The truth behind that emotion is:

One thing I did today that showed strength was:

One small victory I'm celebrating is:

A message to my future self:

**EVENING CENTERING:**

"If all I did today was survive, I did enough"

Tonight my heart needs to hear:

One thing I can release before sleep is:

______________________________________________

______________________________________________

______________________________________________

______________________________________________

______________________________________________

# Daily Freedom Practice

"Healing happens in moments, one breath at a time."

**Day Eleven: ___/___/______**

**MORNING JOURNALING:**

Today I felt trigger by:

______________________________________________

______________________________________________

______________________________________________

______________________________________________

______________________________________________

My body responded with:

_______________________________________________

_______________________________________________

_______________________________________________

_______________________________________________

_______________________________________________

The root emotion I discovered was:

_______________________________________________

_______________________________________________

_______________________________________________

_______________________________________________

_______________________________________________

The truth behind that emotion is:

_______________________________________________

_______________________________________________

_______________________________________________

_______________________________________________

_______________________________________________

One thing I did today that showed strength was:

________________________________________

________________________________________

________________________________________

________________________________________

________________________________________

One small victory I'm celebrating is:

________________________________________

________________________________________

________________________________________

________________________________________

________________________________________

A message to my future self:

________________________________________

________________________________________

________________________________________

________________________________________

________________________________________

## EVENING CENTERING:

"If all I did today was survive, I did enough"

Tonight my heart needs to hear:

_______________________________________________

_______________________________________________

_______________________________________________

_______________________________________________

_______________________________________________

One thing I can release before sleep is:

_______________________________________________

_______________________________________________

_______________________________________________

_______________________________________________

_______________________________________________

# Daily Freedom Practice

"Healing happens in moments, one breath at a time."

**Day Twelve: ___/___/_____**

**MORNING JOURNALING:**

Today I felt trigger by:

____________________________________________

____________________________________________

____________________________________________

____________________________________________

____________________________________________

My body responded with:

____________________________________________

____________________________________________

____________________________________________

____________________________________________

____________________________________________

The root emotion I discovered was:

____________________________________________

____________________________________________

The truth behind that emotion is:

One thing I did today that showed strength was:

One small victory I'm celebrating is:

A message to my future self:

**EVENING CENTERING:**

"If all I did today was survive, I did enough"

Tonight my heart needs to hear:

One thing I can release before sleep is:

_______________________________________________

_______________________________________________

_______________________________________________

_______________________________________________

_______________________________________________

# Daily Freedom Practice

"Healing happens in moments, one breath at a time."

**Day Thirteen: ___/___/______**

**MORNING JOURNALING:**

Today I felt trigger by:

_______________________________________________

_______________________________________________

_______________________________________________

My body responded with:

The root emotion I discovered was:

The truth behind that emotion is:

One thing I did today that showed strength was:

One small victory I'm celebrating is:

A message to my future self:

**EVENING CENTERING:**

"If all I did today was survive, I did enough"

Tonight my heart needs to hear:

One thing I can release before sleep is:

# Daily Freedom Practice:

## Day Fourteen: ___/___/______

### MORNING JOURNALING:

Today I felt trigger by:

______________________________________________________________

______________________________________________________________

______________________________________________________________

______________________________________________________________

______________________________________________________________

My body responded with:

______________________________________________________________

______________________________________________________________

______________________________________________________________

______________________________________________________________

______________________________________________________________

The root emotion I discovered was:

The truth behind that emotion is:

One thing I did today that showed strength was:

One small victory I'm celebrating is:

A message to my future self:

**EVENING CENTERING:**

"If all I did today was survive, I did enough"

Tonight my heart needs to hear:

One thing I can release before sleep is:

# Weekly Review

"Healing becomes visible when I reflect on my journey."

What did I handle better than last week?

What pattern am I starting to understand?

What part of myself came back online this week?

One old wound that softened this week:

One new strength that appeared:

One thing I'm grateful I didn't give up on:

# Daily Freedom Practice

"Healing happens in moments, one breath at a time."

**Day Fifteen: ___/___/______**

**MORNING JOURNALING:**

Today I felt trigger by:

________________________________________

________________________________________

________________________________________

________________________________________

________________________________________

My body responded with:

________________________________________

________________________________________

________________________________________

________________________________________

________________________________________

The root emotion I discovered was:

The truth behind that emotion is:

One thing I did today that showed strength was:

One small victory I'm celebrating is:

A message to my future self:

**EVENING CENTERING:**

"If all I did today was survive, I did enough"

Tonight my heart needs to hear:

______________________________________________

______________________________________________

One thing I can release before sleep is:

______________________________________________

______________________________________________

______________________________________________

______________________________________________

______________________________________________

# Daily Freedom Practice

"Healing happens in moments, one breath at a time."

**Day Sixteen: ___/___/______**

**MORNING JOURNALING:**

Today I felt trigger by:

______________________________________________

______________________________________________

______________________________________________

My body responded with:

The root emotion I discovered was:

The truth behind that emotion is:

One thing I did today that showed strength was:

One small victory I'm celebrating is:

A message to my future self:

## EVENING CENTERING:

"If all I did today was survive, I did enough"

Tonight my heart needs to hear:

One thing I can release before sleep is:

# Daily Freedom Practice

"Healing happens in moments, one breath at a time."

**Day Seventeen: ___/___/______**

**MORNING JOURNALING:**

Today I felt trigger by:

____________________________________________

____________________________________________

____________________________________________

____________________________________________

____________________________________________

My body responded with:

____________________________________________

____________________________________________

____________________________________________

____________________________________________

____________________________________________

The root emotion I discovered was:

________________________________________

________________________________________

________________________________________

________________________________________

________________________________________

The truth behind that emotion is:

________________________________________

________________________________________

________________________________________

________________________________________

________________________________________

One thing I did today that showed strength was:

________________________________________

________________________________________

________________________________________

________________________________________

________________________________________

One small victory I'm celebrating is:

A message to my future self:

**EVENING CENTERING:**

"If all I did today was survive, I did enough"

Tonight my heart needs to hear:

One thing I can release before sleep is:

# Daily Freedom Practice

"Healing happens in moments, one breath at a time."

**Day Eighteen: ___/___/______**

**MORNING JOURNALING:**

Today I felt trigger by:

My body responded with:

The root emotion I discovered was:

The truth behind that emotion is:

One thing I did today that showed strength was:

One small victory I'm celebrating is:

A message to my future self:

## EVENING CENTERING:

"If all I did today was survive, I did enough"

Tonight my heart needs to hear:

One thing I can release before sleep is:

# Daily Freedom Practice

"Healing happens in moments, one breath at a time."

**Day Nineteen: ___/___/______**

**MORNING JOURNALING:**

Today I felt trigger by:

______________________________________________

______________________________________________

______________________________________________

______________________________________________

______________________________________________

My body responded with:

______________________________________________

______________________________________________

______________________________________________

______________________________________________

______________________________________________

The root emotion I discovered was:

________________________________________

________________________________________

________________________________________

________________________________________

________________________________________

The truth behind that emotion is:

________________________________________

________________________________________

________________________________________

________________________________________

________________________________________

One thing I did today that showed strength was:

________________________________________

________________________________________

________________________________________

________________________________________

________________________________________

One small victory I'm celebrating is:

A message to my future self:

**EVENING CENTERING:**

"If all I did today was survive, I did enough"

Tonight my heart needs to hear:

One thing I can release before sleep is:

# Daily Freedom Practice

"Healing happens in moments, one breath at a time."

**Day Twenty: ___/___/______**

**MORNING JOURNALING:**

Today I felt trigger by:

My body responded with:

The root emotion I discovered was:

The truth behind that emotion is:

_______________________________________________

_______________________________________________

_______________________________________________

_______________________________________________

_______________________________________________

One thing I did today that showed strength was:

_______________________________________________

_______________________________________________

_______________________________________________

_______________________________________________

_______________________________________________

One small victory I'm celebrating is:

_______________________________________________

_______________________________________________

_______________________________________________

_______________________________________________

_______________________________________________

A message to my future self:

**EVENING CENTERING:**

"If all I did today was survive, I did enough"

Tonight my heart needs to hear:

One thing I can release before sleep is:

______________________________________________

______________________________________________

______________________________________________

# Daily Freedom Practice

"Healing happens in moments, one breath at a time."

**Day Twenty-One: ___/___/_____**

**MORNING JOURNALING:**

Today I felt trigger by:

______________________________________________

______________________________________________

______________________________________________

______________________________________________

______________________________________________

My body responded with:

______________________________________________

______________________________________________

The root emotion I discovered was:

The truth behind that emotion is:

One thing I did today that showed strength was:

One small victory I'm celebrating is:

A message to my future self:

**EVENING CENTERING:**

"If all I did today was survive, I did enough"

Tonight my heart needs to hear:

One thing I can release before sleep is:

# Weekly Review

"Healing becomes visible when I reflect on my journey."

What did I handle better than last week?

What pattern am I starting to understand?

What part of myself came back online this week?

One old wound that softened this week:

______________________________________________

______________________________________________

______________________________________________

______________________________________________

______________________________________________

One new strength that appeared:

______________________________________________

______________________________________________

______________________________________________

______________________________________________

______________________________________________

One thing I’m grateful I didn’t give up on:

______________________________________________

______________________________________________

______________________________________________

______________________________________________

______________________________________________

# Daily Freedom Practice

"Healing happens in moments, one breath at a time."

**Day Twenty-Two: ___/___/______**

**MORNING JOURNALING:**

Today I felt trigger by:

_____________________________________________

_____________________________________________

_____________________________________________

_____________________________________________

_____________________________________________

My body responded with:

_____________________________________________

_____________________________________________

_____________________________________________

The root emotion I discovered was:

The truth behind that emotion is:

One thing I did today that showed strength was:

One small victory I'm celebrating is:

A message to my future self:

## EVENING CENTERING:

"If all I did today was survive, I did enough"

Tonight my heart needs to hear:

One thing I can release before sleep is:

# Daily Freedom Practice

"Healing happens in moments, one breath at a time."

**Day Twenty-Three: ___/___/______**

## MORNING JOURNALING:

Today I felt trigger by:

My body responded with:

The root emotion I discovered was:

The truth behind that emotion is:

One thing I did today that showed strength was:

One small victory I'm celebrating is:

A message to my future self:

**EVENING CENTERING:**

"If all I did today was survive, I did enough"

Tonight my heart needs to hear:

One thing I can release before sleep is:

______________________________________________

______________________________________________

# Daily Freedom Practice

"Healing happens in moments, one breath at a time."

**Day Twenty-Four: ___/___/______**

**MORNING JOURNALING:**

Today I felt trigger by:

______________________________________________

______________________________________________

______________________________________________

______________________________________________

______________________________________________

My body responded with:

______________________________________________

______________________________________________

______________________________________________

The root emotion I discovered was:

The truth behind that emotion is:

One thing I did today that showed strength was:

One small victory I'm celebrating is:

A message to my future self:

**EVENING CENTERING:**

"If all I did today was survive, I did enough"

Tonight my heart needs to hear:

One thing I can release before sleep is:

# Daily Freedom Practice

"Healing happens in moments, one breath at a time."

**Day Twenty-Five: ___/___/______**

**MORNING JOURNALING:**

Today I felt trigger by:

My body responded with:

The root emotion I discovered was:

The truth behind that emotion is:

One thing I did today that showed strength was:

One small victory I'm celebrating is:

A message to my future self:

## EVENING CENTERING:

"If all I did today was survive, I did enough"

Tonight my heart needs to hear:

One thing I can release before sleep is:

______________________________________________

______________________________________________

# Daily Freedom Practice

"Healing happens in moments, one breath at a time."

**Day Twenty-Six: ___/___/______**

**MORNING JOURNALING:**

Today I felt trigger by:

______________________________________________

______________________________________________

______________________________________________

______________________________________________

______________________________________________

My body responded with:

______________________________________________

______________________________________________

______________________________________________

The root emotion I discovered was:

The truth behind that emotion is:

One thing I did today that showed strength was:

One small victory I'm celebrating is:

A message to my future self:

**EVENING CENTERING:**

"If all I did today was survive, I did enough"

Tonight my heart needs to hear:

_______________________________________________

_______________________________________________

_______________________________________________

_______________________________________________

_______________________________________________

One thing I can release before sleep is:

_______________________________________________

_______________________________________________

_______________________________________________

_______________________________________________

_______________________________________________

# Daily Freedom Practice

"Healing happens in moments, one breath at a time."

**Day Twenty-Seven: ___/___/______**

## MORNING JOURNALING:

Today I felt trigger by:

My body responded with:

The root emotion I discovered was:

The truth behind that emotion is:

One thing I did today that showed strength was:

One small victory I'm celebrating is:

A message to my future self:

**EVENING CENTERING:**

"If all I did today was survive, I did enough"

Tonight my heart needs to hear:

One thing I can release before sleep is:

______________________________________________

______________________________________________

______________________________________________

______________________________________________

______________________________________________

# Daily Freedom Practice

"Healing happens in moments, one breath at a time."

**Day Twenty-Eight: ___/___/______**

**MORNING JOURNALING:**

Today I felt trigger by:

______________________________________________

______________________________________________

______________________________________________

______________________________________________

______________________________________________

My body responded with:

______________________________________________

______________________________________________

______________________________________________

______________________________________________

______________________________________________

The root emotion I discovered was:

______________________________________________

______________________________________________

______________________________________________

______________________________________________

______________________________________________

The truth behind that emotion is:

______________________________________________

______________________________________________

______________________________________________

______________________________________________

______________________________________________

One thing I did today that showed strength was:

One small victory I'm celebrating is:

A message to my future self:

## EVENING CENTERING:

"If all I did today was survive, I did enough"

Tonight my heart needs to hear:

_______________________________________________

_______________________________________________

_______________________________________________

_______________________________________________

_______________________________________________

One thing I can release before sleep is:

_______________________________________________

_______________________________________________

_______________________________________________

_______________________________________________

_______________________________________________

# Weekly Review

"Healing becomes visible when I reflect on my journey."

What did I handle better than last week?

________________________________________________________________

________________________________________________________________

________________________________________________________________

________________________________________________________________

________________________________________________________________

What pattern am I starting to understand?

________________________________________________________________

________________________________________________________________

________________________________________________________________

________________________________________________________________

________________________________________________________________

What part of myself came back online this week?

________________________________________________________________

________________________________________________________________

________________________________________________________________

One old wound that softened this week:

One new strength that appeared:

One thing I'm grateful I didn't give up on:

# 2nd Monthly Breakthrough Page

"Breakthroughs are quiet moments of clarity. Not explosions."

What I see changing in me:

Old wounds that shifted:

New strengths I'm noticing:

People who feel safe for me now:

People I am learning to distance from:

My biggest win this month:

What I want to focus on next month:

# Daily Freedom Practice

"Healing happens in moments, one breath at a time."

**Day One: ___/___/______**

**MORNING JOURNALING:**

Today I felt trigger by:

____________________________________________

____________________________________________

____________________________________________

____________________________________________

____________________________________________

My body responded with:

____________________________________________

____________________________________________

____________________________________________

____________________________________________

____________________________________________

The root emotion I discovered was:

The truth behind that emotion is:

One thing I did today that showed strength was:

One small victory I'm celebrating is:

_______________________________________________

_______________________________________________

_______________________________________________

_______________________________________________

_______________________________________________

A message to my future self:

_______________________________________________

_______________________________________________

_______________________________________________

_______________________________________________

_______________________________________________

**EVENING CENTERING:**

"If all I did today was survive, I did enough"

Tonight my heart needs to hear:

_______________________________________________

_______________________________________________

________________________________________

________________________________________

________________________________________

One thing I can release before sleep is:

________________________________________

________________________________________

________________________________________

________________________________________

________________________________________

# Daily Freedom Practice

"Healing happens in moments, one breath at a time."

**Day Two: ___/___/______**

## MORNING JOURNALING:

Today I felt trigger by:

________________________________________

________________________________________

My body responded with:

The root emotion I discovered was:

The truth behind that emotion is:

One thing I did today that showed strength was:

One small victory I'm celebrating is:

A message to my future self:

## EVENING CENTERING:

"If all I did today was survive, I did enough"

Tonight my heart needs to hear:

One thing I can release before sleep is:

# Daily Freedom Practice

"Healing happens in moments, one breath at a time."

**Day Three: ___/___/______**

**MORNING JOURNALING:**

Today I felt trigger by:

_______________________________________________

_______________________________________________

_______________________________________________

_______________________________________________

_______________________________________________

My body responded with:

_______________________________________________

_______________________________________________

_______________________________________________

_______________________________________________

_______________________________________________

The root emotion I discovered was:

_______________________________________________

_______________________________________________

_______________________________________________

_______________________________________________

_______________________________________________

The truth behind that emotion is:

_______________________________________________

_______________________________________________

_______________________________________________

_______________________________________________

_______________________________________________

One thing I did today that showed strength was:

_______________________________________________

_______________________________________________

_______________________________________________

_______________________________________________

_______________________________________________

One small victory I'm celebrating is:

________________________________________

A message to my future self:

## EVENING CENTERING:

"If all I did today was survive, I did enough"

Tonight my heart needs to hear:

One thing I can release before sleep is:

# Daily Freedom Practice

"Healing happens in moments, one breath at a time."

**Day Four: ___/___/______**

**MORNING JOURNALING:**

Today I felt trigger by:

My body responded with:

The root emotion I discovered was:

The truth behind that emotion is:

One thing I did today that showed strength was:

One small victory I'm celebrating is:

A message to my future self:

**EVENING CENTERING:**

"If all I did today was survive, I did enough"

Tonight my heart needs to hear:

One thing I can release before sleep is:

# Daily Freedom Practice

"Healing happens in moments, one breath at a time."

**Day Five: ___/___/______**

**MORNING JOURNALING:**

Today I felt trigger by:

________________________________________

________________________________________

________________________________________

________________________________________

________________________________________

My body responded with:

________________________________________

________________________________________

________________________________________

________________________________________

________________________________________

The root emotion I discovered was:

The truth behind that emotion is:

One thing I did today that showed strength was:

One small victory I'm celebrating is:

______________________________________________

______________________________________________

______________________________________________

______________________________________________

______________________________________________

A message to my future self:

______________________________________________

______________________________________________

______________________________________________

______________________________________________

______________________________________________

## EVENING CENTERING:

"If all I did today was survive, I did enough"

Tonight my heart needs to hear:

One thing I can release before sleep is:

# Daily Freedom Practice

"Healing happens in moments, one breath at a time."

**Day Six: ___/___/______**

**MORNING JOURNALING:**

Today I felt trigger by:

My body responded with:

The root emotion I discovered was:

The truth behind that emotion is:

One thing I did today that showed strength was:

One small victory I'm celebrating is:

A message to my future self:

## EVENING CENTERING:

"If all I did today was survive, I did enough"

Tonight my heart needs to hear:

One thing I can release before sleep is:

______________________________________________

______________________________________________

______________________________________________

# Daily Freedom Practice

"Healing happens in moments, one breath at a time."

**Day Seven: ___/___/______**

**MORNING JOURNALING:**

Today I felt trigger by:

______________________________________________

______________________________________________

______________________________________________

______________________________________________

______________________________________________

My body responded with:

______________________________________________

______________________________________________

The root emotion I discovered was:

The truth behind that emotion is:

One thing I did today that showed strength was:

One small victory I'm celebrating is:

A message to my future self:

**EVENING CENTERING:**

"If all I did today was survive, I did enough"

Tonight my heart needs to hear:

_______________________________________________

_______________________________________________

_______________________________________________

_______________________________________________

_______________________________________________

One thing I can release before sleep is:

_______________________________________________

_______________________________________________

_______________________________________________

_______________________________________________

_______________________________________________

# Weekly Review

"Healing becomes visible when I reflect on my journey."

What did I handle better than last week?

What pattern am I starting to understand?

What part of myself came back online this week?

One old wound that softened this week:

One new strength that appeared:

One thing I'm grateful I didn't give up on:

# Daily Freedom Practice

"Healing happens in moments, one breath at a time."

**Day Eight: ___/___/______**

**MORNING JOURNALING:**

Today I felt trigger by:

________________________________________

________________________________________

________________________________________

________________________________________

________________________________________

My body responded with:

________________________________________

________________________________________

________________________________________

The root emotion I discovered was:

The truth behind that emotion is:

One thing I did today that showed strength was:

One small victory I'm celebrating is:

A message to my future self:

## EVENING CENTERING:

"If all I did today was survive, I did enough"

Tonight my heart needs to hear:

One thing I can release before sleep is:

# Daily Freedom Practice

"Healing happens in moments, one breath at a time."

**Day Nine: ___/___/______**

**MORNING JOURNALING:**

Today I felt trigger by:

My body responded with:

The root emotion I discovered was:

The truth behind that emotion is:

One thing I did today that showed strength was:

One small victory I'm celebrating is:

A message to my future self:

## EVENING CENTERING:

"If all I did today was survive, I did enough"

Tonight my heart needs to hear:

One thing I can release before sleep is:

______________________________________________

______________________________________________

# Daily Freedom Practice

"Healing happens in moments, one breath at a time."

**Day Ten: ___/___/______**

**MORNING JOURNALING:**

Today I felt trigger by:

______________________________________________

______________________________________________

______________________________________________

______________________________________________

______________________________________________

My body responded with:

______________________________________________

______________________________________________

______________________________________________

The root emotion I discovered was:

The truth behind that emotion is:

One thing I did today that showed strength was:

One small victory I'm celebrating is:

A message to my future self:

**EVENING CENTERING:**

"If all I did today was survive, I did enough"

Tonight my heart needs to hear:

_______________________________________________

_______________________________________________

_______________________________________________

_______________________________________________

_______________________________________________

One thing I can release before sleep is:

_______________________________________________

_______________________________________________

_______________________________________________

_______________________________________________

_______________________________________________

# Daily Freedom Practice

"Healing happens in moments, one breath at a time."

**Day Eleven: ___/___/______**

**MORNING JOURNALING:**

Today I felt trigger by:

My body responded with:

The root emotion I discovered was:

The truth behind that emotion is:

One thing I did today that showed strength was:

One small victory I'm celebrating is:

A message to my future self:

## EVENING CENTERING:

"If all I did today was survive, I did enough"

Tonight my heart needs to hear:

One thing I can release before sleep is:

______________________________________________

______________________________________________

# Daily Freedom Practice

"Healing happens in moments, one breath at a time."

**Day Twelve: ___/___/______**

**MORNING JOURNALING:**

Today I felt trigger by:

______________________________________________

______________________________________________

______________________________________________

______________________________________________

______________________________________________

My body responded with:

______________________________________________

______________________________________________

______________________________________________

The root emotion I discovered was:

The truth behind that emotion is:

One thing I did today that showed strength was:

One small victory I'm celebrating is:

A message to my future self:

**EVENING CENTERING:**

"If all I did today was survive, I did enough"

Tonight my heart needs to hear:

________________________________________________

________________________________________________

________________________________________________

________________________________________________

________________________________________________

One thing I can release before sleep is:

________________________________________________

________________________________________________

________________________________________________

________________________________________________

________________________________________________

# Daily Freedom Practice

"Healing happens in moments, one breath at a time."

**Day Thirteen: ___/___/______**

**MORNING JOURNALING:**

Today I felt trigger by:

________________________________________

________________________________________

________________________________________

________________________________________

________________________________________

My body responded with:

________________________________________

________________________________________

________________________________________

________________________________________

________________________________________

The root emotion I discovered was:

________________________________________

________________________________________

________________________________________

The truth behind that emotion is:

One thing I did today that showed strength was:

One small victory I'm celebrating is:

A message to my future self:

**EVENING CENTERING:**

"If all I did today was survive, I did enough"

Tonight my heart needs to hear:

One thing I can release before sleep is:

______________________________________________

______________________________________________

______________________________________________

______________________________________________

______________________________________________

# Daily Freedom Practice:

**Day Fourteen: ___/___/______**

**MORNING JOURNALING:**

Today I felt trigger by:

______________________________________________

______________________________________________

______________________________________________

______________________________________________

______________________________________________

My body responded with:

The root emotion I discovered was:

The truth behind that emotion is:

One thing I did today that showed strength was:

________________________________________

________________________________________

________________________________________

________________________________________

________________________________________

One small victory I'm celebrating is:

________________________________________

________________________________________

________________________________________

________________________________________

________________________________________

A message to my future self:

________________________________________

________________________________________

________________________________________

________________________________________

________________________________________

**EVENING CENTERING:**

"If all I did today was survive, I did enough"

Tonight my heart needs to hear:

______________________________________________

______________________________________________

______________________________________________

______________________________________________

______________________________________________

One thing I can release before sleep is:

______________________________________________

______________________________________________

______________________________________________

______________________________________________

______________________________________________

# Weekly Review

"Healing becomes visible when I reflect on my journey."

What did I handle better than last week?

____________________________________________

____________________________________________

____________________________________________

____________________________________________

____________________________________________

What pattern am I starting to understand?

____________________________________________

____________________________________________

____________________________________________

____________________________________________

____________________________________________

What part of myself came back online this week?

____________________________________________

____________________________________________

One old wound that softened this week:

One new strength that appeared:

One thing I'm grateful I didn't give up on:

______________________________________________

______________________________________________

______________________________________________

# Daily Freedom Practice

"Healing happens in moments, one breath at a time."

**Day Fifteen: ___/___/_____**

**MORNING JOURNALING:**

Today I felt trigger by:

______________________________________________

______________________________________________

______________________________________________

______________________________________________

______________________________________________

My body responded with:

The root emotion I discovered was:

The truth behind that emotion is:

One thing I did today that showed strength was:

__________________________________________________

__________________________________________________

__________________________________________________

__________________________________________________

__________________________________________________

One small victory I'm celebrating is:

__________________________________________________

__________________________________________________

__________________________________________________

__________________________________________________

__________________________________________________

A message to my future self:

__________________________________________________

__________________________________________________

__________________________________________________

__________________________________________________

__________________________________________________

**EVENING CENTERING:**

"If all I did today was survive, I did enough"

Tonight my heart needs to hear:

________________________________________

________________________________________

________________________________________

________________________________________

________________________________________

One thing I can release before sleep is:

________________________________________

________________________________________

________________________________________

________________________________________

________________________________________

# Daily Freedom Practice

"Healing happens in moments, one breath at a time."

**Day Sixteen: ___/___/_____**

**MORNING JOURNALING:**

Today I felt trigger by:

____________________________________________

____________________________________________

____________________________________________

____________________________________________

____________________________________________

My body responded with:

____________________________________________

____________________________________________

____________________________________________

____________________________________________

____________________________________________

The root emotion I discovered was:

____________________________________________

____________________________________________

The truth behind that emotion is:

One thing I did today that showed strength was:

One small victory I'm celebrating is:

A message to my future self:

**EVENING CENTERING:**

"If all I did today was survive, I did enough"

Tonight my heart needs to hear:

One thing I can release before sleep is:

______________________________________________

______________________________________________

______________________________________________

______________________________________________

______________________________________________

# Daily Freedom Practice

"Healing happens in moments, one breath at a time."

**Day Seventeen: ___/___/______**

**MORNING JOURNALING:**

Today I felt trigger by:

______________________________________________

______________________________________________

______________________________________________

______________________________________________

______________________________________________

My body responded with:

The root emotion I discovered was:

The truth behind that emotion is:

One thing I did today that showed strength was:

One small victory I'm celebrating is:

A message to my future self:

**EVENING CENTERING:**

"If all I did today was survive, I did enough"

Tonight my heart needs to hear:

______________________________________________

______________________________________________

______________________________________________

______________________________________________

______________________________________________

One thing I can release before sleep is:

______________________________________________

______________________________________________

______________________________________________

______________________________________________

______________________________________________

# Daily Freedom Practice

"Healing happens in moments, one breath at a time."

**Day Eighteen: ___/___/_____**

## MORNING JOURNALING:

Today I felt trigger by:

______________________________________________

______________________________________________

______________________________________________

______________________________________________

______________________________________________

My body responded with:

______________________________________________

______________________________________________

______________________________________________

______________________________________________

______________________________________________

The root emotion I discovered was:

______________________________________________

______________________________________________

The truth behind that emotion is:

One thing I did today that showed strength was:

One small victory I'm celebrating is:

A message to my future self:

## EVENING CENTERING:

"If all I did today was survive, I did enough"

Tonight my heart needs to hear:

One thing I can release before sleep is:

_______________________________________________

_______________________________________________

_______________________________________________

_______________________________________________

_______________________________________________

# Daily Freedom Practice

"Healing happens in moments, one breath at a time."

**Day Nineteen: ___/___/______**

**MORNING JOURNALING:**

Today I felt trigger by:

_______________________________________________

_______________________________________________

_______________________________________________

_______________________________________________

_______________________________________________

My body responded with:

________________________________________

________________________________________

________________________________________

________________________________________

________________________________________

The root emotion I discovered was:

________________________________________

________________________________________

________________________________________

________________________________________

________________________________________

The truth behind that emotion is:

________________________________________

________________________________________

________________________________________

________________________________________

________________________________________

One thing I did today that showed strength was:

One small victory I'm celebrating is:

A message to my future self:

## EVENING CENTERING:

"If all I did today was survive, I did enough"

Tonight my heart needs to hear:

______________________________________________

______________________________________________

______________________________________________

______________________________________________

______________________________________________

One thing I can release before sleep is:

______________________________________________

______________________________________________

______________________________________________

______________________________________________

______________________________________________

# Daily Freedom Practice

"Healing happens in moments, one breath at a time."

**Day Twenty: ___/___/______**

**MORNING JOURNALING:**

Today I felt trigger by:

________________________________________

________________________________________

________________________________________

________________________________________

________________________________________

My body responded with:

________________________________________

________________________________________

________________________________________

________________________________________

________________________________________

The root emotion I discovered was:

________________________________________

________________________________________

________________________________________

________________________________________

________________________________________

The truth behind that emotion is:

________________________________________

________________________________________

________________________________________

________________________________________

________________________________________

One thing I did today that showed strength was:

________________________________________

________________________________________

________________________________________

________________________________________

________________________________________

One small victory I'm celebrating is:

______________________________________________

______________________________________________

______________________________________________

______________________________________________

______________________________________________

A message to my future self:

______________________________________________

______________________________________________

______________________________________________

______________________________________________

______________________________________________

**EVENING CENTERING:**

"If all I did today was survive, I did enough"

Tonight my heart needs to hear:

______________________________________________

______________________________________________

________________________________________________

________________________________________________

________________________________________________

One thing I can release before sleep is:

________________________________________________

________________________________________________

________________________________________________

________________________________________________

________________________________________________

# Daily Freedom Practice

“Healing happens in moments, one breath at a time.”

**Day Twenty-One: ___/___/______**

## MORNING JOURNALING:

Today I felt trigger by:

________________________________________________

________________________________________________

My body responded with:

The root emotion I discovered was:

The truth behind that emotion is:

One thing I did today that showed strength was:

One small victory I'm celebrating is:

A message to my future self:

**EVENING CENTERING:**

"If all I did today was survive, I did enough"

Tonight my heart needs to hear:

One thing I can release before sleep is:

# Weekly Review

"Healing becomes visible when I reflect on my journey."

What did I handle better than last week?

_______________________________________________

_______________________________________________

_______________________________________________

_______________________________________________

_______________________________________________

What pattern am I starting to understand?

_______________________________________________

_______________________________________________

_______________________________________________

_______________________________________________

_______________________________________________

What part of myself came back online this week?

_______________________________________________

_______________________________________________

_______________________________________________

_______________________________________________

_______________________________________________

One old wound that softened this week:

_______________________________________________

_______________________________________________

_______________________________________________

_______________________________________________

_______________________________________________

One new strength that appeared:

_______________________________________________

_______________________________________________

_______________________________________________

_______________________________________________

_______________________________________________

One thing I'm grateful I didn't give up on:

_______________________________________________

_______________________________________________

_______________________________________________

_______________________________________________

_______________________________________________

# Daily Freedom Practice

"Healing happens in moments, one breath at a time."

**Day Twenty-Two: ___/___/______**

**MORNING JOURNALING:**

Today I felt trigger by:

_______________________________________________

_______________________________________________

_______________________________________________

My body responded with:

The root emotion I discovered was:

The truth behind that emotion is:

One thing I did today that showed strength was:

One small victory I'm celebrating is:

A message to my future self:

## EVENING CENTERING:

"If all I did today was survive, I did enough"

Tonight my heart needs to hear:

One thing I can release before sleep is:

# Daily Freedom Practice

"Healing happens in moments, one breath at a time."

**Day Twenty-Three: ___/___/______**

**MORNING JOURNALING:**

Today I felt trigger by:

______________________________________________

______________________________________________

______________________________________________

______________________________________________

______________________________________________

My body responded with:

______________________________________________

______________________________________________

______________________________________________

______________________________________________

______________________________________________

The root emotion I discovered was:

________________________________________

________________________________________

________________________________________

________________________________________

________________________________________

The truth behind that emotion is:

________________________________________

________________________________________

________________________________________

________________________________________

________________________________________

One thing I did today that showed strength was:

________________________________________

________________________________________

________________________________________

________________________________________

________________________________________

One small victory I'm celebrating is:

________________________________________

A message to my future self:

________________________________________

**EVENING CENTERING:**

"If all I did today was survive, I did enough"

Tonight my heart needs to hear:

One thing I can release before sleep is:

# Daily Freedom Practice

"Healing happens in moments, one breath at a time."

**Day Twenty-Four: ___/___/______**

**MORNING JOURNALING:**

Today I felt trigger by:

My body responded with:

The root emotion I discovered was:

The truth behind that emotion is:

One thing I did today that showed strength was:

One small victory I'm celebrating is:

A message to my future self:

**EVENING CENTERING:**

"If all I did today was survive, I did enough"

Tonight my heart needs to hear:

One thing I can release before sleep is:

# Daily Freedom Practice

"Healing happens in moments, one breath at a time."

**Day Twenty-Five: ___/___/______**

**MORNING JOURNALING:**

Today I felt trigger by:

______________________________________________

______________________________________________

______________________________________________

______________________________________________

______________________________________________

My body responded with:

______________________________________________

______________________________________________

______________________________________________

______________________________________________

______________________________________________

The root emotion I discovered was:

_______________________________________________________________

The truth behind that emotion is:

_______________________________________________________________

One thing I did today that showed strength was:

_______________________________________________________________

One small victory I'm celebrating is:

_______________________________________________

_______________________________________________

_______________________________________________

_______________________________________________

_______________________________________________

A message to my future self:

_______________________________________________

_______________________________________________

_______________________________________________

_______________________________________________

_______________________________________________

**EVENING CENTERING:**

"If all I did today was survive, I did enough"

Tonight my heart needs to hear:

One thing I can release before sleep is:

# Daily Freedom Practice

"Healing happens in moments, one breath at a time."

**Day Twenty-Six: ___/___/______**

**MORNING JOURNALING:**

Today I felt trigger by:

My body responded with:

The root emotion I discovered was:

The truth behind that emotion is:

One thing I did today that showed strength was:

One small victory I'm celebrating is:

A message to my future self:

## EVENING CENTERING:

"If all I did today was survive, I did enough"

Tonight my heart needs to hear:

One thing I can release before sleep is:

______________________________________________

______________________________________________

# Daily Freedom Practice

"Healing happens in moments, one breath at a time."

**Day Twenty-Seven: ___/___/______**

**MORNING JOURNALING:**

Today I felt trigger by:

______________________________________________

______________________________________________

______________________________________________

______________________________________________

______________________________________________

My body responded with:

The root emotion I discovered was:

The truth behind that emotion is:

One thing I did today that showed strength was:

________________________________________

________________________________________

________________________________________

________________________________________

________________________________________

One small victory I’m celebrating is:

________________________________________

________________________________________

________________________________________

________________________________________

________________________________________

A message to my future self:

________________________________________

________________________________________

________________________________________

________________________________________

________________________________________

**EVENING CENTERING:**

"If all I did today was survive, I did enough"

Tonight my heart needs to hear:

_______________________________________________

_______________________________________________

_______________________________________________

_______________________________________________

_______________________________________________

One thing I can release before sleep is:

_______________________________________________

_______________________________________________

_______________________________________________

_______________________________________________

_______________________________________________

# Daily Freedom Practice

"Healing happens in moments, one breath at a time."

## Day Twenty-Eight: ___/___/______

### MORNING JOURNALING:

Today I felt trigger by:

______________________________________________

______________________________________________

______________________________________________

______________________________________________

______________________________________________

My body responded with:

______________________________________________

______________________________________________

______________________________________________

______________________________________________

______________________________________________

The root emotion I discovered was:

______________________________________________

______________________________________________

The truth behind that emotion is:

One thing I did today that showed strength was:

One small victory I'm celebrating is:

A message to my future self:

## EVENING CENTERING:

"If all I did today was survive, I did enough"

Tonight my heart needs to hear:

One thing I can release before sleep is:

# Weekly Review

"Healing becomes visible when I reflect on my journey."

What did I handle better than last week?

What pattern am I starting to understand?

What part of myself came back online this week?

One old wound that softened this week:

One new strength that appeared:

_______________________________________________

_______________________________________________

_______________________________________________

_______________________________________________

_______________________________________________

One thing I'm grateful I didn't give up on:

_______________________________________________

_______________________________________________

_______________________________________________

_______________________________________________

_______________________________________________

# 3rd Monthly Breakthrough Page

"Breakthroughs are quiet moments of clarity. Not explosions."

What I see changing in me:

Old wounds that shifted:

New strengths I'm noticing:

People who feel safe for me now:

People I am learning to distance from:

My biggest win this month:

What I want to focus on next month:

My body responded with:

The root emotion I discovered was:

The truth behind that emotion is:

One thing I did today that showed strength was:

One small victory I'm celebrating is:

A message to my future self:

**EVENING CENTERING:**

"If all I did today was survive, I did enough"

Tonight my heart needs to hear:

One thing I can release before sleep is:

________________________________________

________________________________________

________________________________________

________________________________________

________________________________________

# My Freedom Letter

"I survived moments that tried to break me. I am learning to live beyond them."

Who I was when I started:

_______________________________________________

_______________________________________________

_______________________________________________

_______________________________________________

_______________________________________________

_______________________________________________

_______________________________________________

_______________________________________________

_______________________________________________

_______________________________________________

_______________________________________________

_______________________________________________

_______________________________________________

## Who I am now:

## Who I refuse to be again:

Who I choose to become next:

# Closing Words

**“Freedom is not the absence of pain – it is the presence of myself”**

I am reclaiming what was always mine: my story, my voice, my peace, my future.

## *Inspirational Quotes Throughout this Journal:*

"Courage is not the absence of fear – it is walking forward even when fear is present."

"My scars are proof that I survived, and that survival is strength."

"Healing is not linear; it is a mosaic of my brave choices, small victories, and quiet resilience."

"Even in darkness, the smallest light matters. I am my own light."

***CONGRADULATIONS!***

***WE CONQUERED***

***OUR PTSD***

***TOGETHER!!!***

**OV – See More Live More!**

**And Again, a *Special Thank You* to My Best Friend!**

www.ingramcontent.com/pod-product-compliance
Lightning Source LLC
LaVergne TN
LVHW081400110826
845149LV00010B/1628

* 9 7 9 8 9 9 2 1 4 1 5 1 1 *